What Is Soft?

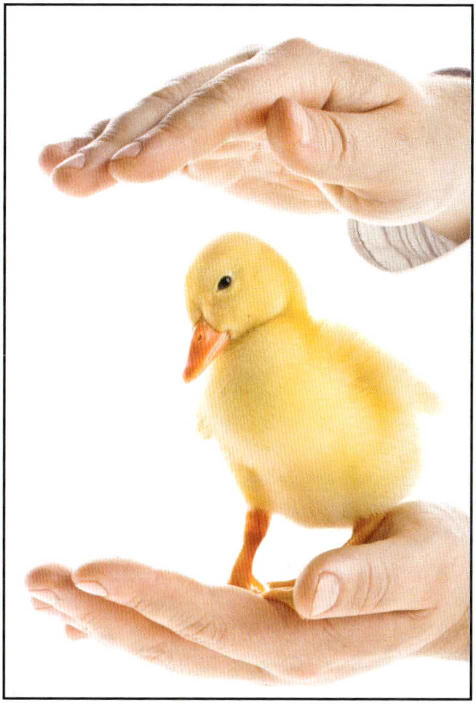

written by Pam Holden

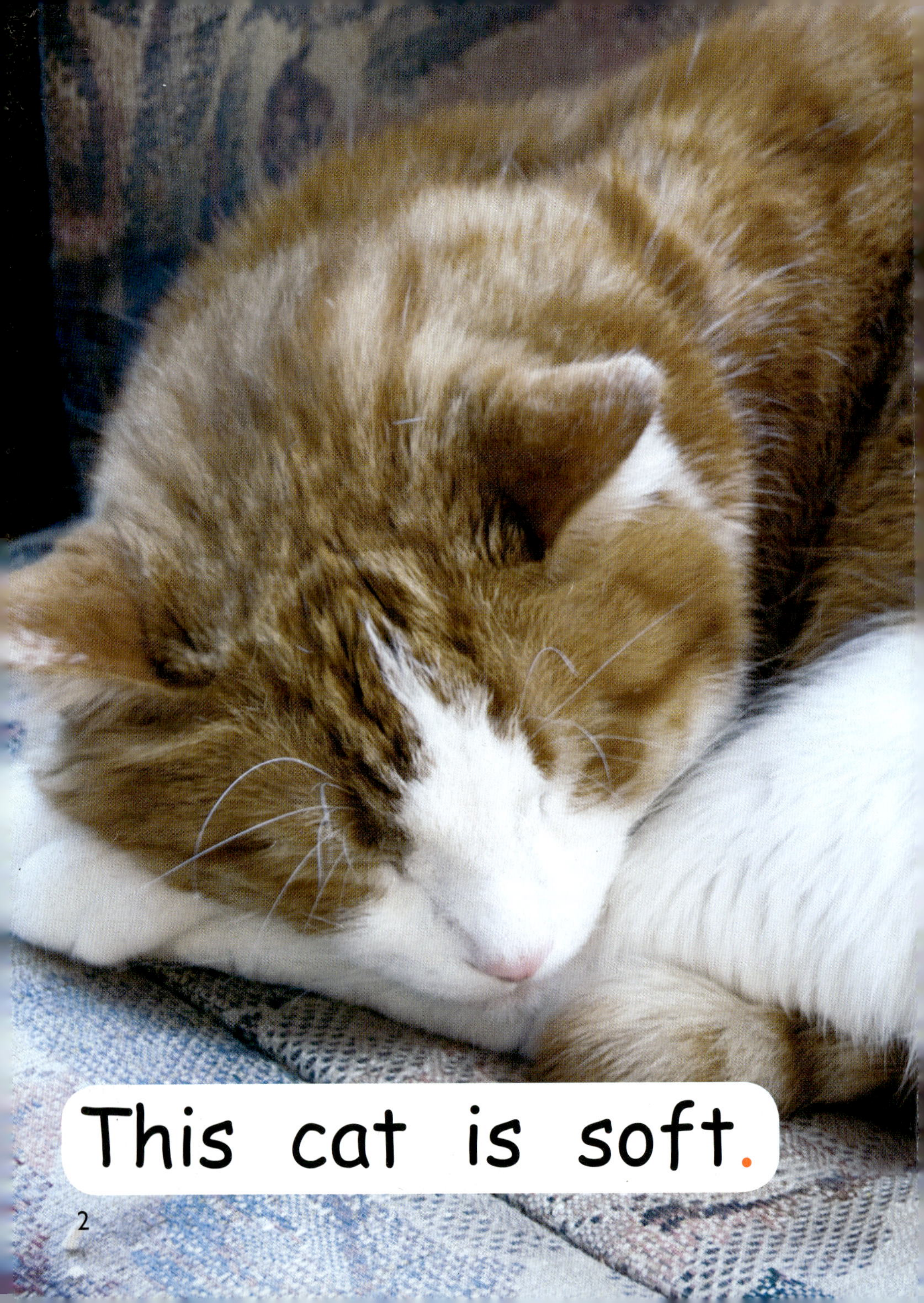

This cat is soft.

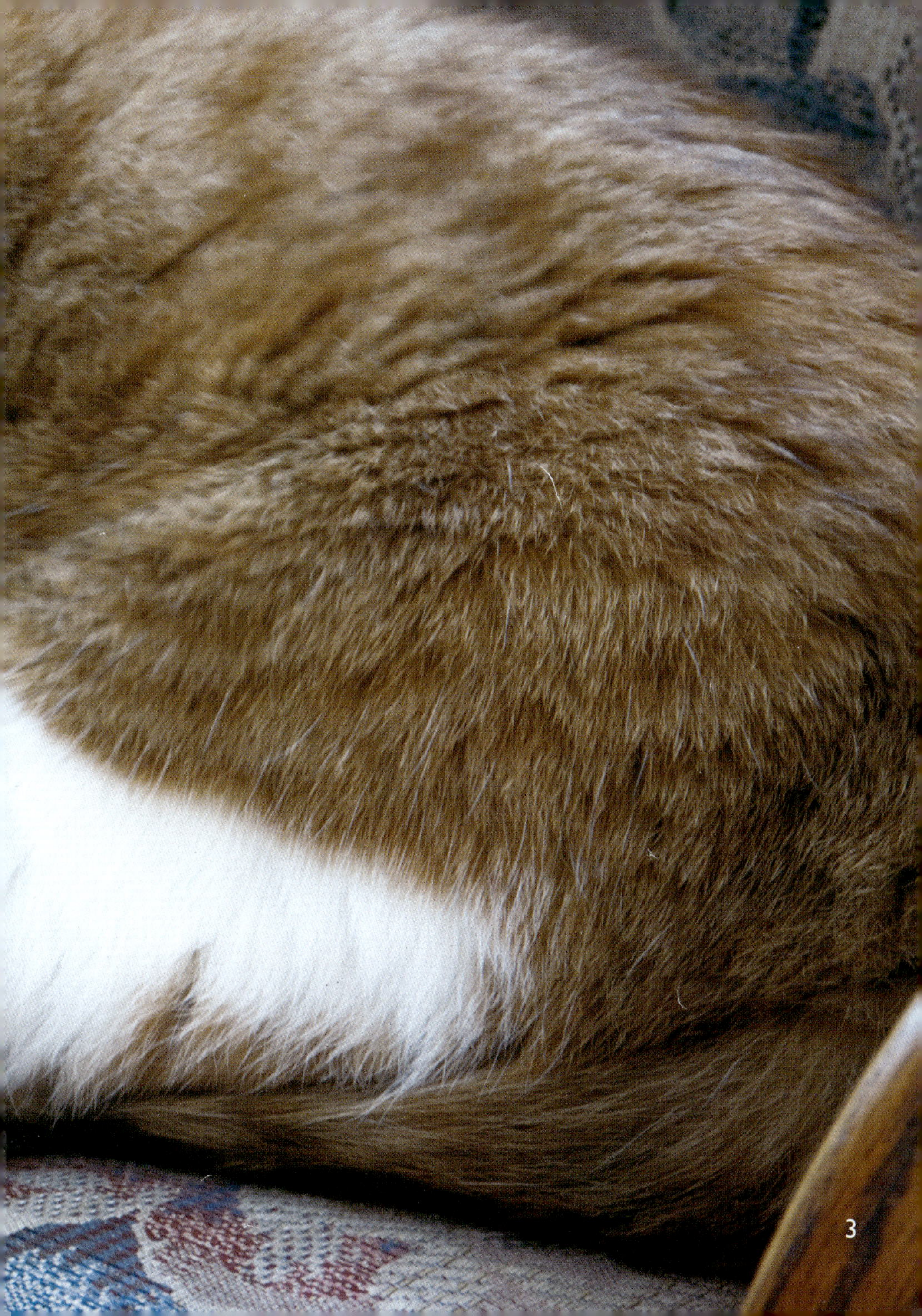

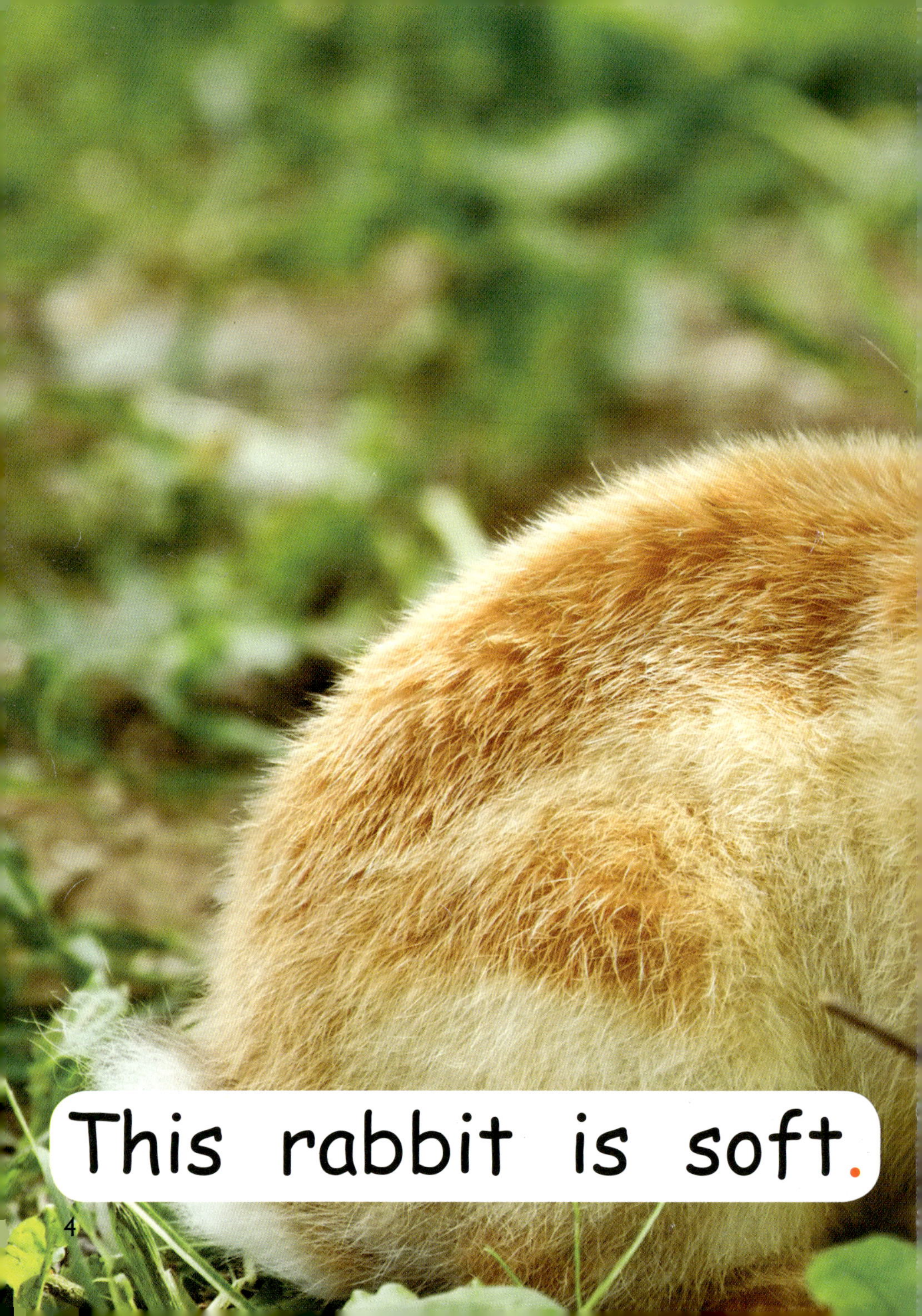

This rabbit is soft.

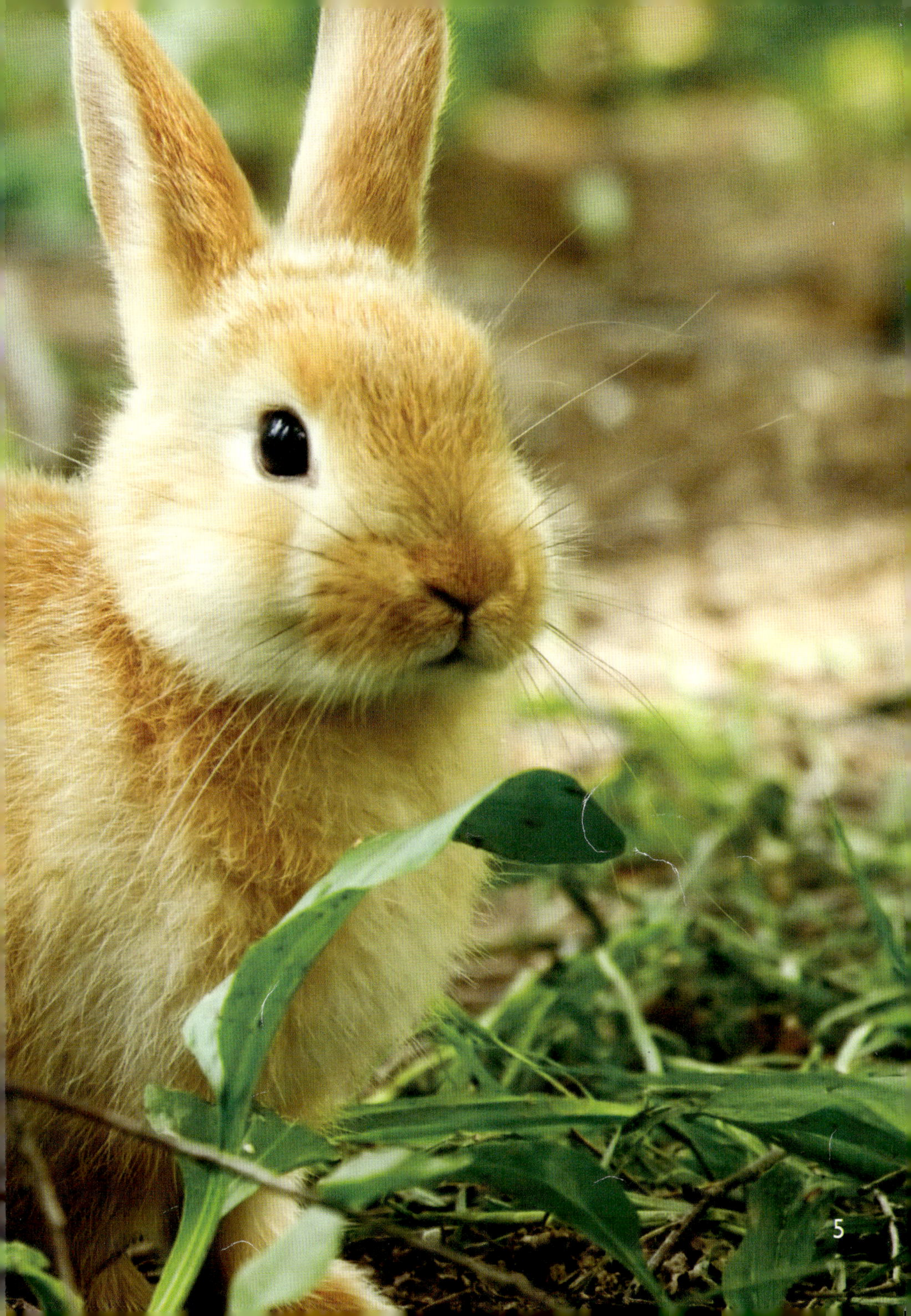

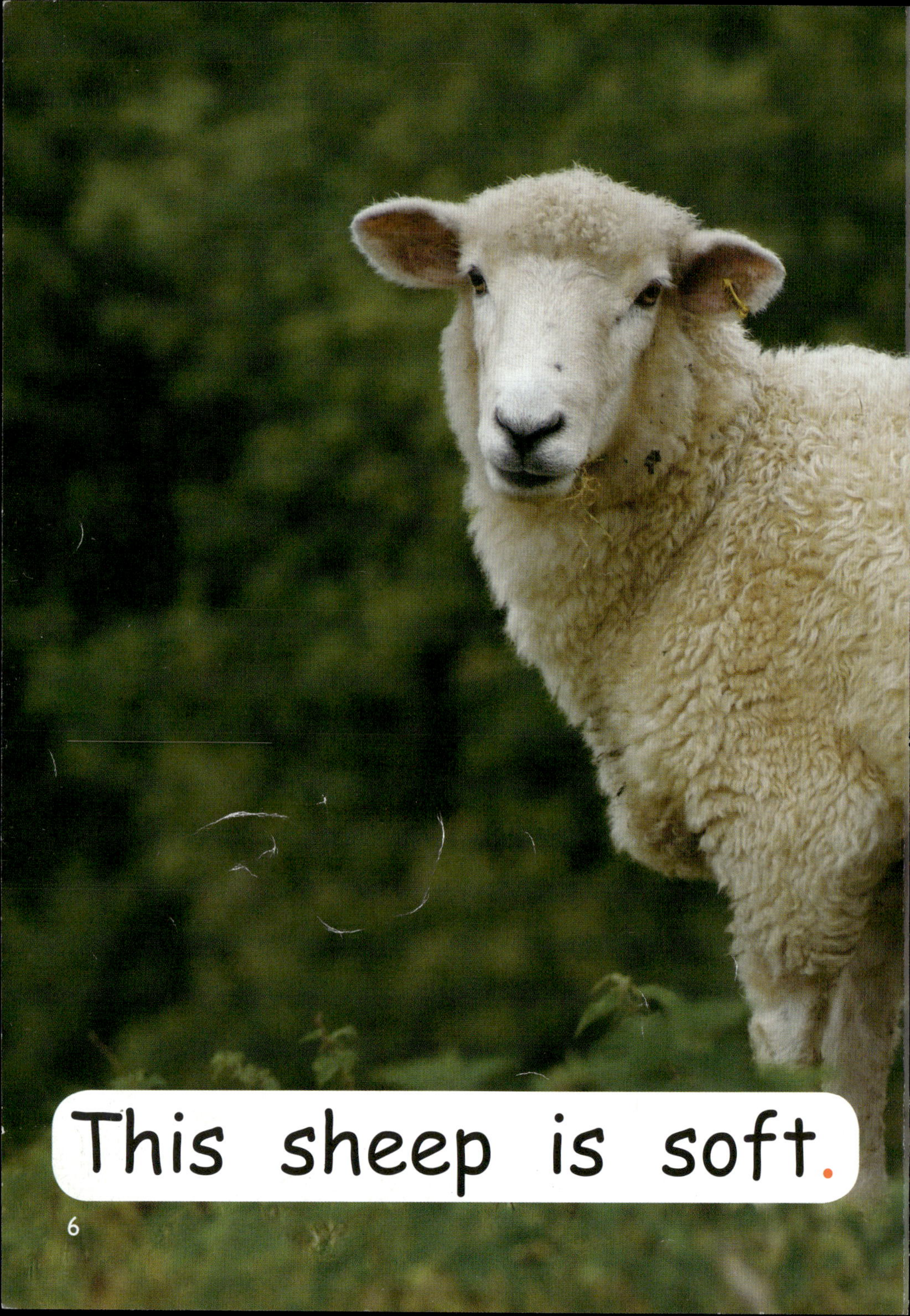

This sheep is soft.

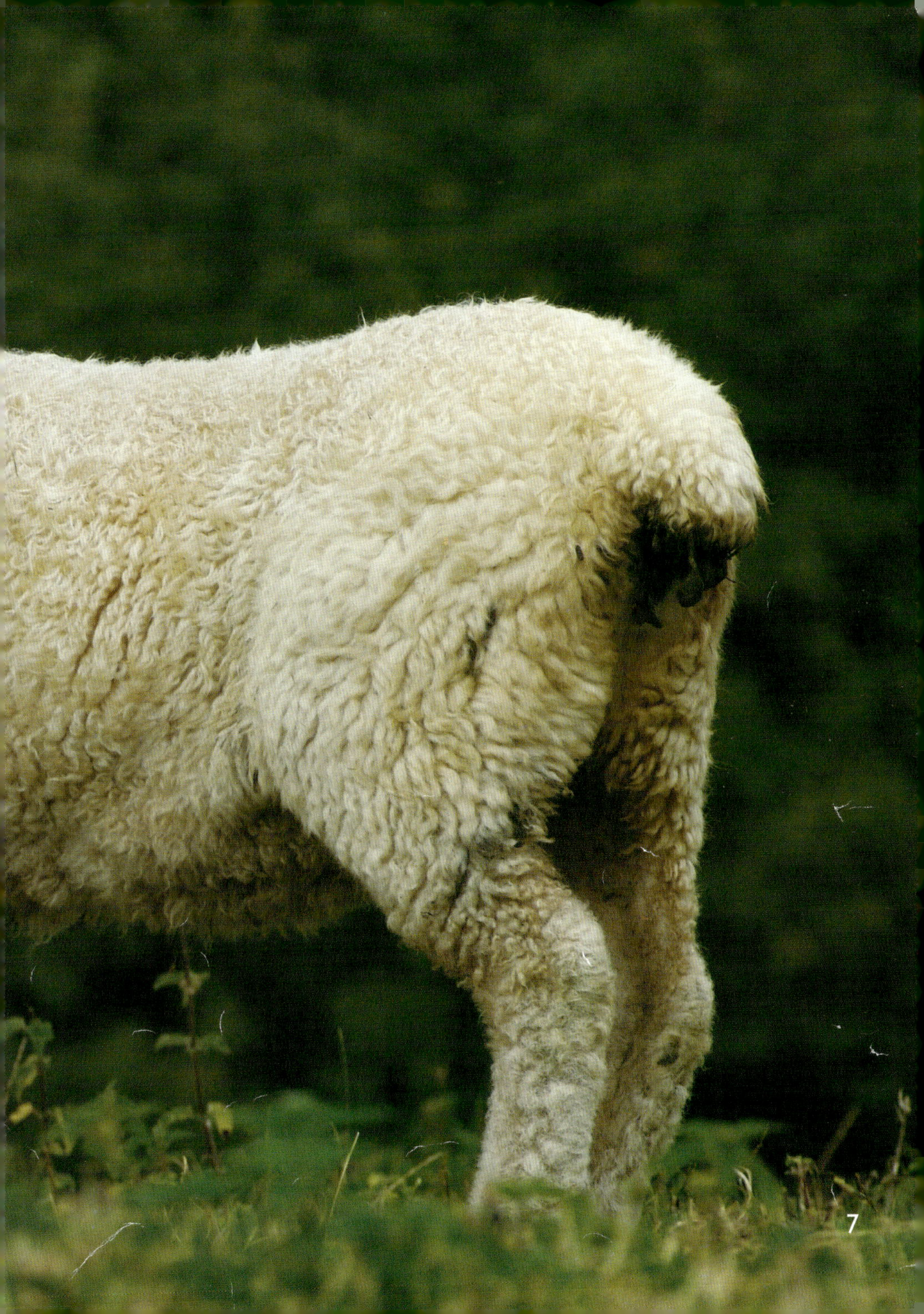

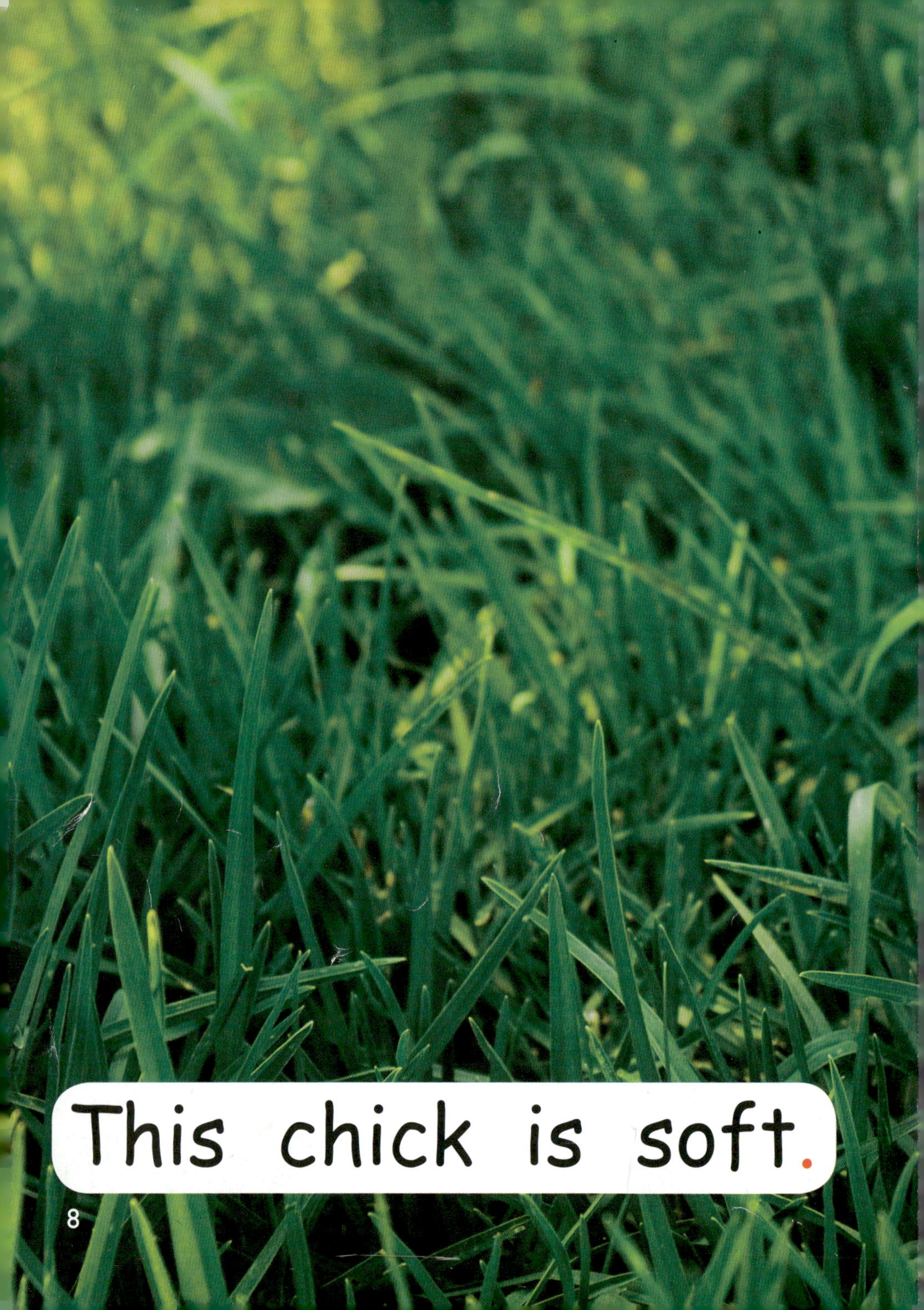

This chick is soft.

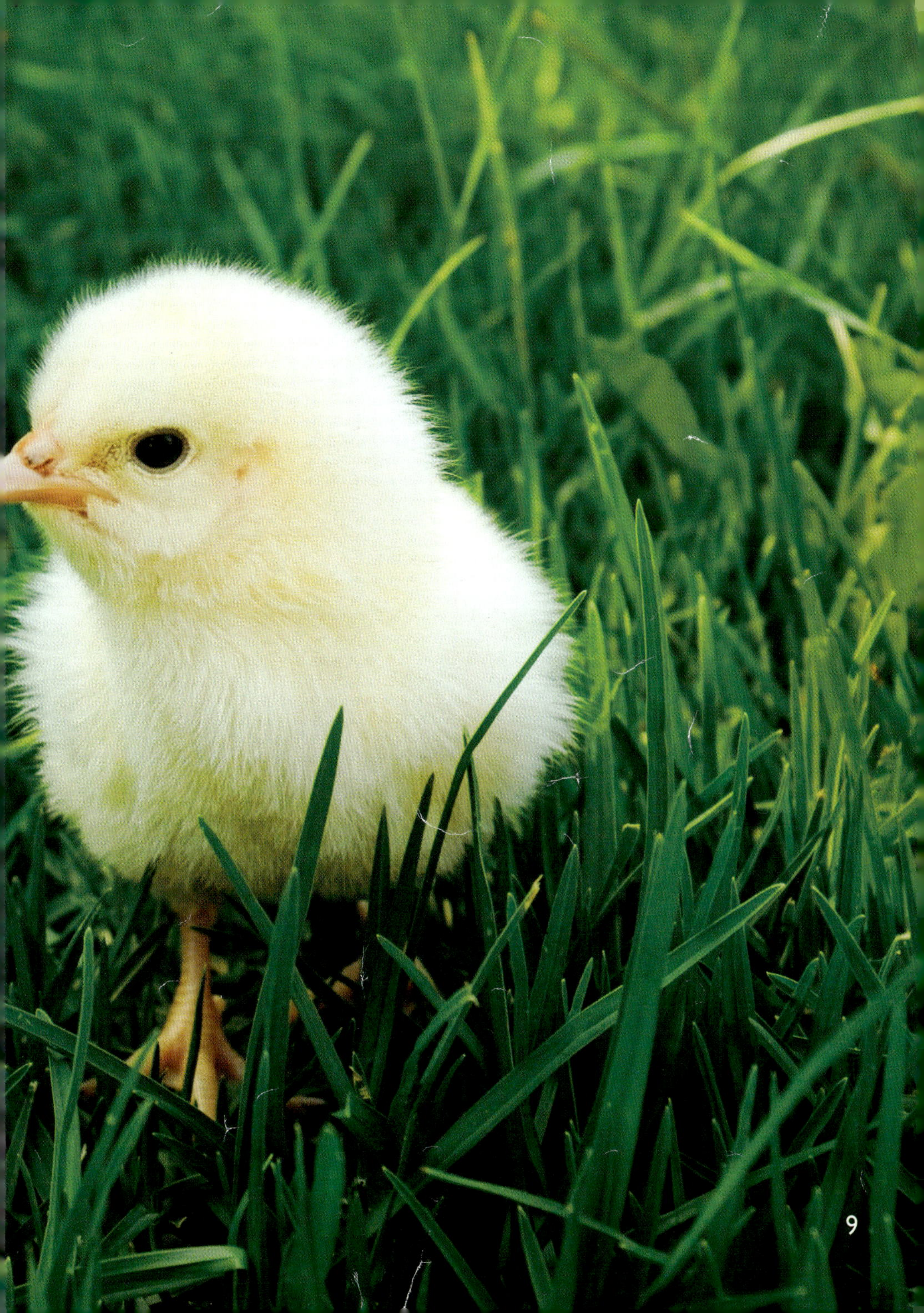

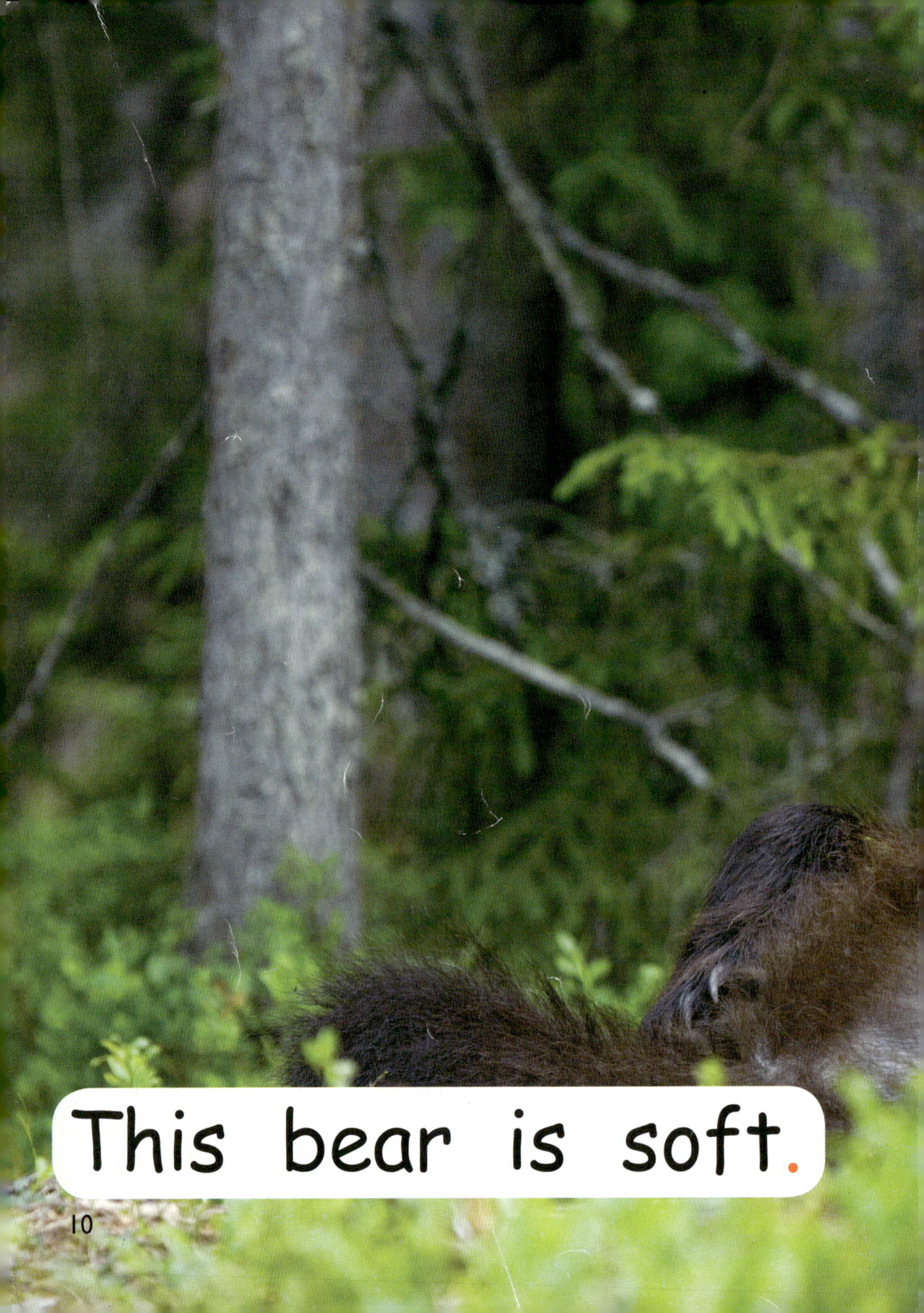

This bear is soft.

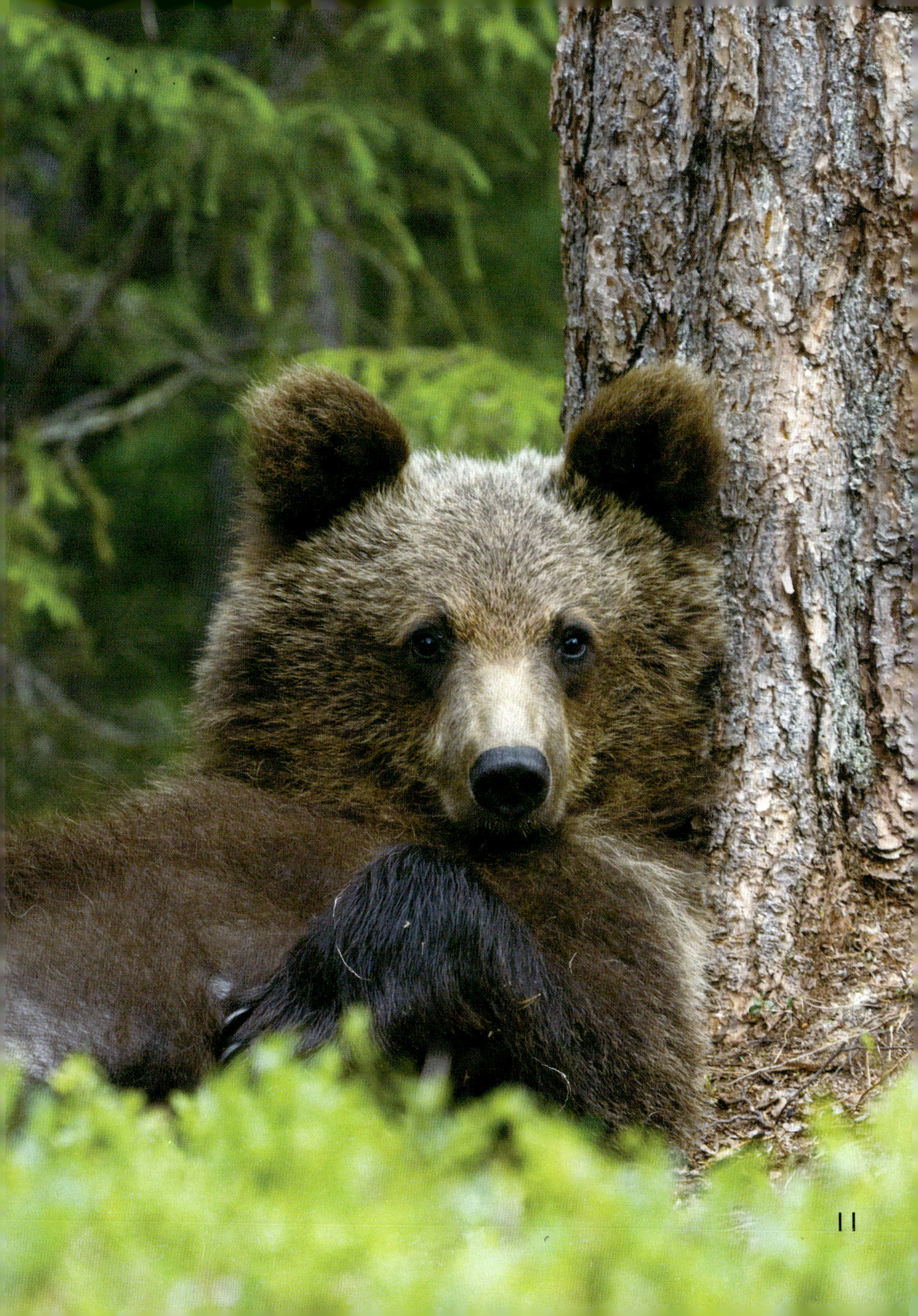

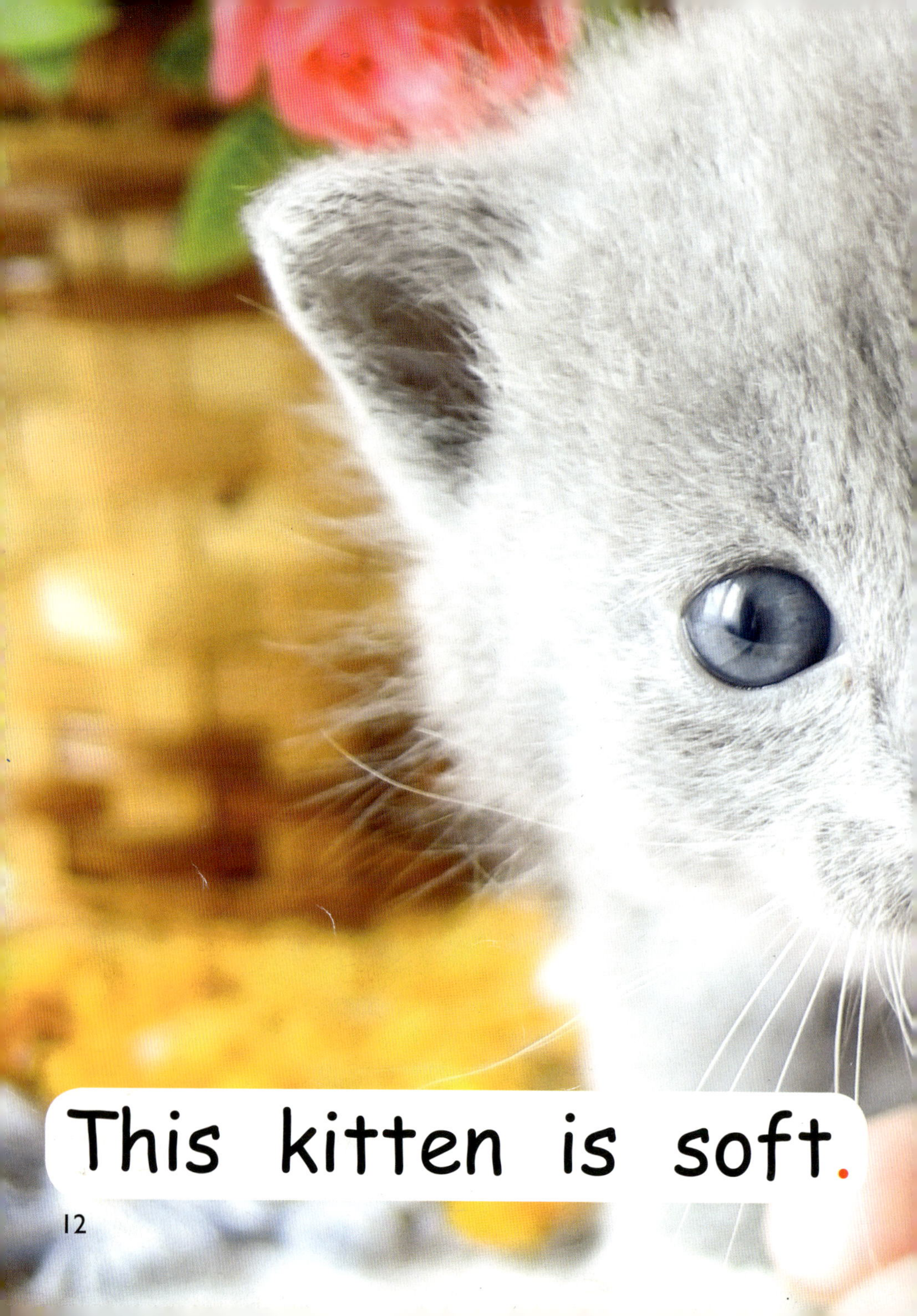

This kitten is soft.

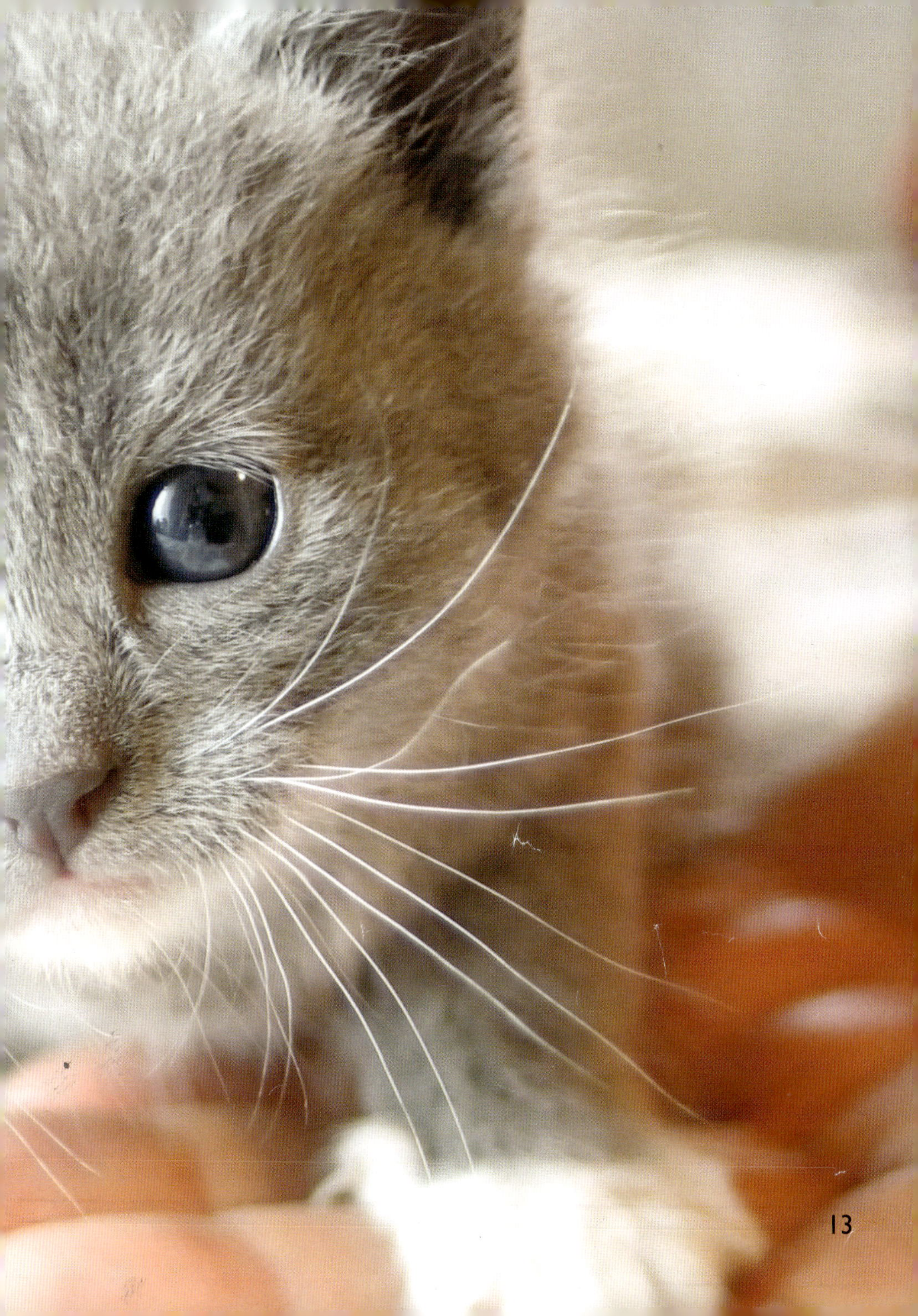

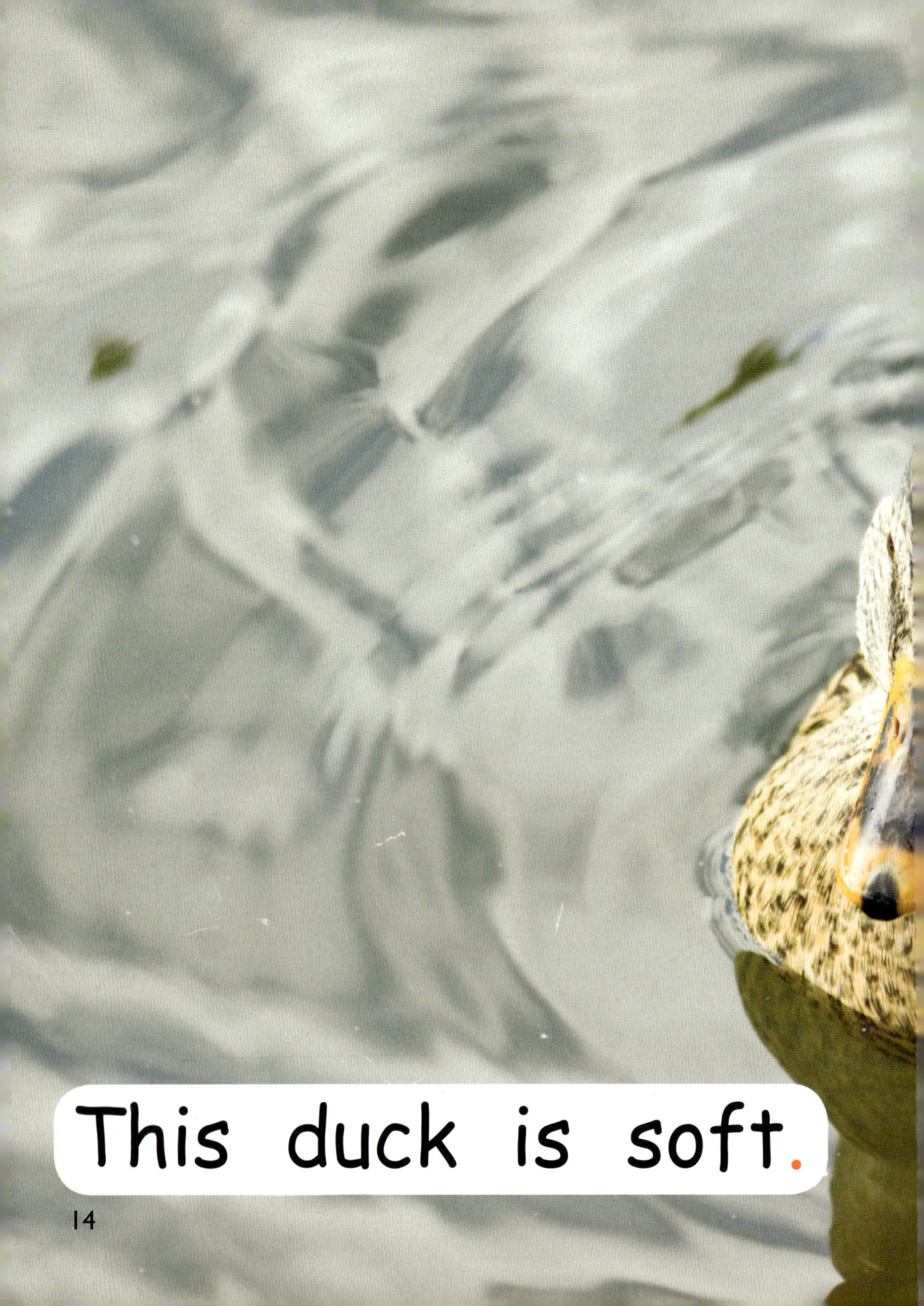

This duck is soft.

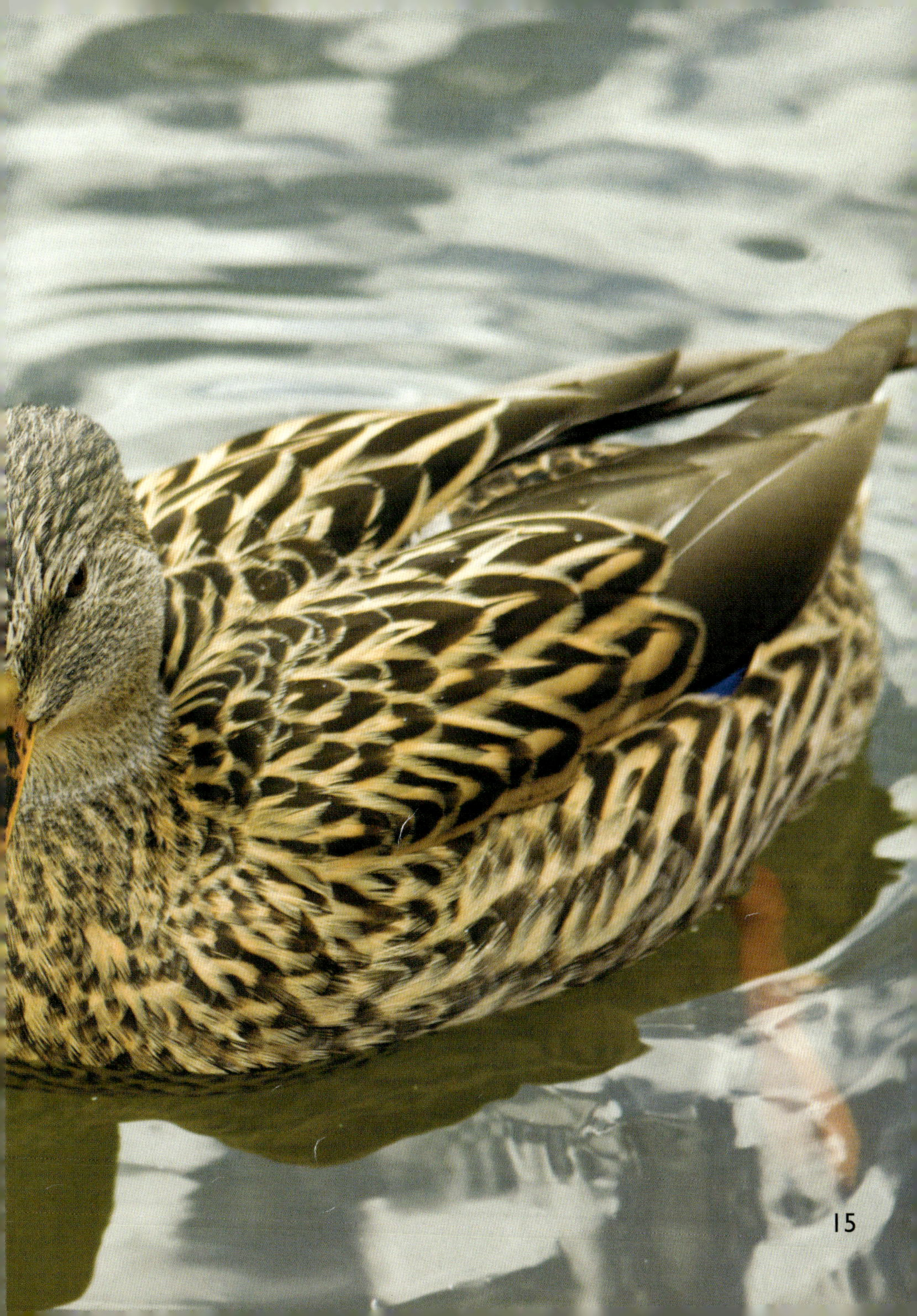

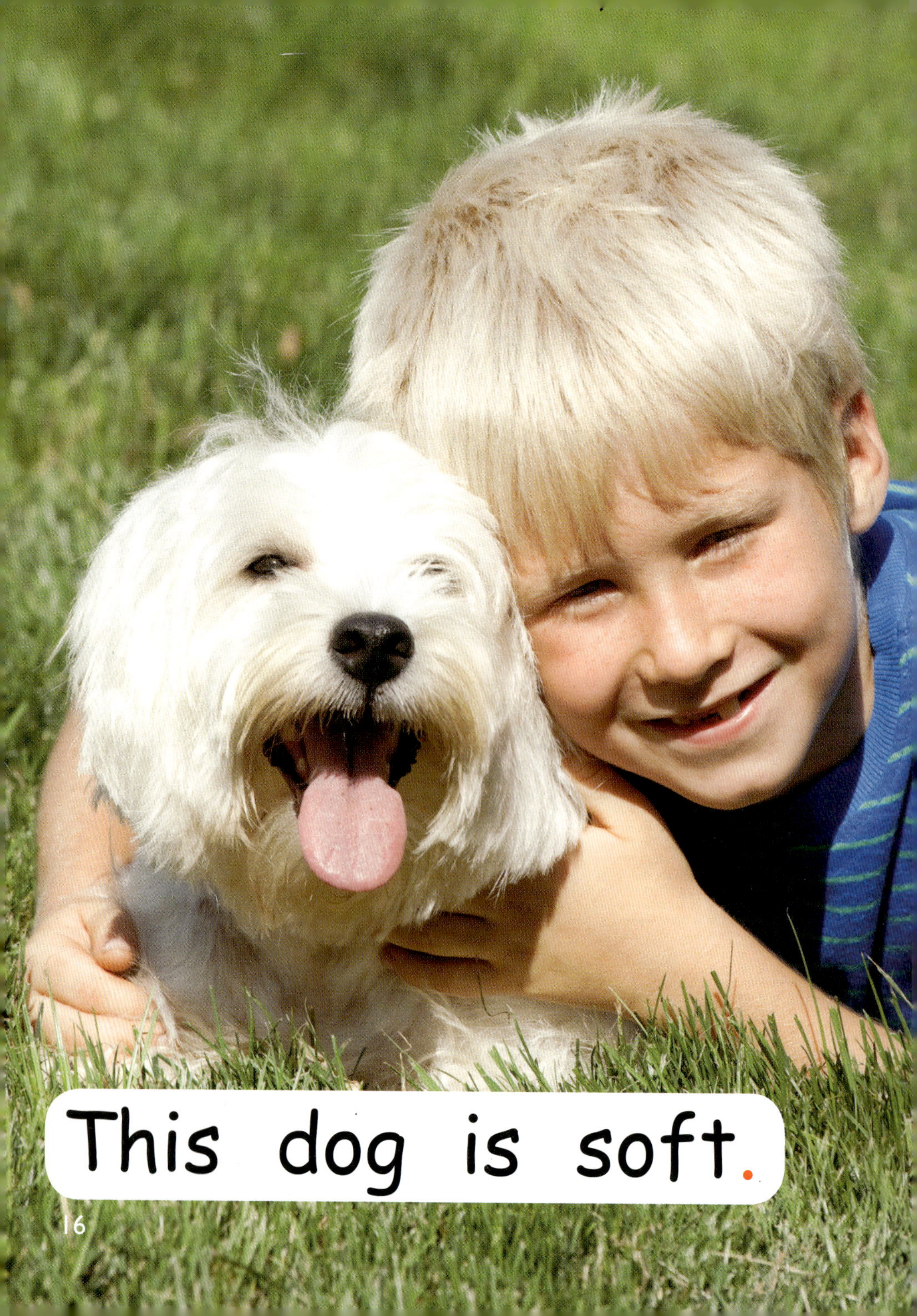

This dog is soft.